Our City Holidays

Teacher's Boo'

by Julia Timlin
Pupil's Book by Jillian Pc

Contents

PEARSON
Longman
Edinburgh Gate
Harlow, Essex

London

Guided Reading

Key Objectives

- Read recounts and begin to recognise generic structure, e.g. ordered sequence of events, use of words like 'first', 'next', 'after', 'when'.
- Locate parts of the text that give particular information, including labelled diagrams and charts.
- Read on sight the eight high frequency words from the Reception Year list.

The teacher will need four sets of Copymaster 1 with the words and pictures cut out, a piece of paper to cover over the teacher's set of words and pictures, and a whiteboard and marker pen.

Reception high frequency words: 'a', 'and', 'I', 'in', 'on', 'the', 'to', 'went'.

Introduction

- Talk about places the children have visited. Make a list on the whiteboard of names of places that can be used during the guided writing follow-up session.
- Look at the front and back covers of the book. Read the title to the group. Establish the content. *This book is about children's visits to lots of different cities in the UK.*
- Show the children the map and point out London. This is the city we are reading about today.
- Show the high frequency words in the text and ask the children to read them.
- Give out one book to each pair and support the children in finding page 2. Use the illustrations and questions as cues to draw out the key vocabulary. *Where is the hippo?*
- Make sure the children understand that the book is written in the first person. *The child is telling us what they did and where they went.* Demonstrate by reading the first line of the text: 'I went to London.'
- **Strategy Check:** Remind the children to use the pictures to help with difficult words. Show how to point to the initial sound and say it out loud.

Reading and Discussion

- Ask the children to read each page with a partner. Refer to the strategy check.
- Check each pair and support with strategies as necessary.
- When they have read the text together, ask one partner to be the teacher and the other to read the text. *Help the reader like I have done by reminding them to look at the pictures or point to the first sound of the word.*
- The partners can then take turns to read to each other and play the part of the teacher.

Returning to the Text for Evaluation and Analysis

- Finally, review the partner reading and the strategies they used to read the words.
- Jumble up the teacher's set of words and pictures from **Copymaster 1**, and through discussion sequence the events of the text. *How do we know this comes last?* Point out the use of the word 'then', which means it comes after. Cover over the teacher's words. Give each pair their own jumbled set and ask them to sequence in the correct order. Uncover and self-check with main sequenced cards.

London

Guided Writing

Key Objectives

- Write simple recounts linked to topics of interest/study using the language of texts read as a model for own writing.
- Through reading and writing, reinforce knowledge of the term 'sentence' from previous terms.

Task

Write a sequence of sentences to match the pictures. Use the structure of the 'London' text as a model.

Each child will need *Our City Holidays* and Copymaster 2.
The teacher will need a whiteboard and marker pen.

Introduction

- Together, read the 'London' text again.
- Ask the children to put the books away before doing the task.
- Give each child a copy of **Copymaster 2**. Discuss the pictures and match them to the words. Remind the group of the picture cue strategy. Ask questions to enable the group to generate the full sentences. *What always goes at the end of the sentence?*
- Demonstrate the first sentence on the whiteboard, pausing to encourage the children to help with the capital letter, spellings and full stop. Reread the sentence together.
- Check proper understanding of the task before moving into the writing.

Children Writing Individually

- For each sentence with missing words, go through this procedure:
- – Say the complete sentence aloud, e.g. 'I went to …?' (place of group choice taken from the list generated in guided reading).
  – Tell the children the words you want them to write.
  – Say each word, separating out the phonemes where appropriate, e.g. 'w-e-n-t'. Encourage the children to say the phonemes to themselves as they write the letters.
  – Where it is a high frequency word children should write the word independently. If there are any difficulties, write the word on your whiteboard and take the child/children through the 'look, say, cover, write, check' process.
  – Repeat the whole sentence aloud. *Have you remembered what goes at the end?*

Evaluation

- Each child should read one sentence in sequence to the group.
- Review the spelling of each word they have written in the session.
- Reflect on progress made in the session. *Which words can you write now? Which words were difficult?* Volunteers could demonstrate on the whiteboard.

Suggested Independent Activities

- Record on tape your recount of a school visit or holiday.
- With an adult or partner, try to find some more information about London or your chosen seaside town, in your school library.
- Write a sequence of sentences about a school visit.

A Visit to London

zoo

hippo

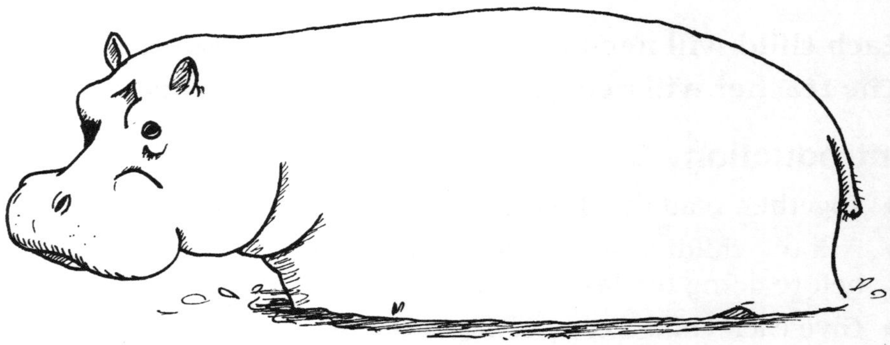

Big Ben and Tower Bridge

London Eye

My Seaside Holiday in ________________

_ _____ __ __________

_ _____ __ ___ beach

_ _____ __ donkey

__ _____ sand

_ _____ __ ___ train

_ ___ boats ___ planes

Then _ _____ __

___ swingboats

Cardiff

Guided Reading

Key Objectives

- Read recounts and begin to recognise generic structure, e.g. ordered sequence of events, use of words like 'first', 'next', 'after', 'when'.
- Locate parts of the text that give particular information, including labelled diagrams and charts.
- Read on sight the six high frequency words from the Reception Year list.

The teacher will need the words and sentences cut out from Copymaster 3.

Reception high frequency words: 'a', 'I', 'in', 'the', 'to', 'went'.

Introduction

- Recap on the visit to London before modelling finding 'Cardiff' for the group. Get them to follow.
- *Who was telling us about their visit to London last time?* Remind them that this book is recounted in the first person. *It is written as though I am the person telling the reader.*
- Show the group where Cardiff is on the map. Discuss what is there – the stadium, the castle, things in the castle. Point to each name as they are discussed.
- *Who is in Cardiff with the person telling the story?*
- Remind the children of the strategies you want them to focus on.
- Read the high frequency words together and then leave them on the table as support.
- **Strategy Check:** Remind the children to use the pictures to help with difficult words. Show how to point to the initial sound and say it out loud.

Reading and Discussion

- Ask the children to read in pairs.
- Check each pair and support with strategies as necessary.
- When they have read the text together, ask one partner to be the teacher (as in the last reading session) and the other to read the text. *Help the reader as I have done, by reminding them to look at the pictures or point to the first sound of the word.*
- The partners can then take turns to read to each other and play the part of the teacher.

Returning to the Text for Evaluation and Analysis

- Review the partner reading and the strategies they used to read the words.
- Put the sequence words from Copymaster 3 in the middle of the table and read them with the group: 'First', 'Next', 'After that', 'Then'.
- Ask the children in pairs to help you to put the sentences from the text [Copymaster 3] in the right order by referring to *Our City Holidays*.
- When completed, read the whole text together, including the sequencing words.
- If there is time, ask the children to make up some sentences that include the words, e.g. 'First, I got my coat. Next I went out to play.'

Cardiff

Guided Writing

Key Objectives

- Use the language and features of non-fiction texts, e.g. captions for pictures.
- Through reading and writing, reinforce knowledge of the term 'sentence' from previous terms.

Task

Write a sentence caption for each of the castle pictures to explain what it is.

Each child will need *Our City Holidays* and Copymaster 4.
The teacher will need a whiteboard and marker pen.

Introduction

- Reread the 'Cardiff' text and ask the children to follow in their books. Look at the pictures and their captions. Discuss.
- Give out **Copymaster 4**. Explain to the children that they are going to write captions. Clarify the term and why a picture needs to have one. Talk through each section. Keep referring back to the text for vocabulary and ideas. *We need to explain each picture using a full sentence. What makes a sentence?* A capital letter, a full stop, and that it makes complete sense.
- Look at each picture, clarify what it is and take suggestions for what to write, e.g. 'This is ______.' 'Here is ______.' 'This is a picture of ______.'
- All the difficult vocabulary needed appears somewhere in the text or on **Copymaster 4**.

Children Writing Individually

- Children write the captions.
- Encourage them to use a range of strategies to find and use the words they want. *Can you find that word in the text? Can you say the phonemes in that word? Does it look right? Try to remember the shape of the word.* Use the whiteboard for spelling checks.
- Remind the children to check for mistakes by reading their finished sentence. *Does it make sense? Have you remembered the capital letter and the full stop?*

Evaluation

- Share aspects of their individual work, highlighting points of support offered and successful strategies employed to spell words correctly and write full sentences.

Suggested Independent Activities

- Use the sequencing words on **Copymaster 3** to write a recount of a holiday or school event.
- Find more information about castles from the Internet and reference books.
- Draw a picture of a castle and label the different parts.
- Practise writing the key words on a whiteboard. Put them into full sentences.

A Visit to Cardiff

First	Next
After that	Then

I went to Cardiff. I went to stay with my grandad.

we went to a football match.

we went to Cardiff Castle.

we saw the clock tower.

Cardiff Captions

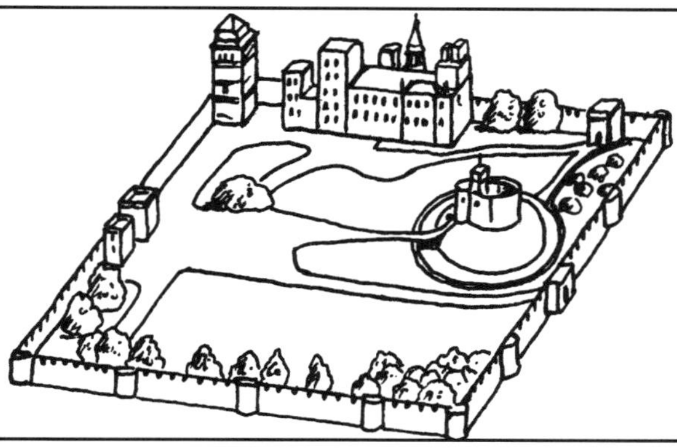

Cardiff Castle	keep
walls	clock tower

Belfast

Guided Reading

Key Objectives

- Read recounts and begin to recognise generic structure, e.g. ordered sequence of events, use of words like 'first', 'next', 'after', 'when'.
- Locate parts of the text that give particular information, including labelled diagrams and charts.

Each pair of children will need *Our City Holidays.*
The teacher will need Copymaster 5 already cut up and stuck onto separate cards, and a whiteboard and marker pen.

Introduction

- Introduce the book by talking about places the children have visited. Make a list on the whiteboard of names of places that can be used during the guided writing sessions.
- Look at the front and back covers of the book. Read the title to the group. Establish the content. *This book is about children's visits to lots of different cities in the UK.*
- Show the children the map and find Belfast. *This is the city we are reading about today.*
- Give out one book to each pair and ask them to find page 10. *The title is Belfast.* Look through the illustrations and introduce the unfamiliar vocabulary: 'Superbowl', 'Candy Factory', 'museum', 'skeletons', 'treasure', 'Irish'. Ask the children to use their phonic knowledge to decipher 'sweets' and 'animal'.
- Make sure the children understand that this book is written in the first person. *The child is telling us what they did, and when they are joined by a friend the 'I' becomes 'We'.* Demonstrate by reading the first line of the text: 'I went to Belfast', 'We went to …'
- **Strategy Check:** Remind the children to use the pictures to help with difficult words. Demonstrate how predicting, leaving a gap and rereading is a useful reading strategy.

Reading and Discussion

- Ask the children to read each page with a partner. Refer to the strategy checks.
- Check each pair as they read and prompt and support with strategies as necessary.
- When they have read the text together, ask one partner to be the teacher and the other to read the text. *Help the reader as I have done by reminding them to look at the pictures or predict a word, leave a gap and then reread the sentence.*
- The partners can then take turns to read to each other and play the part of the teacher.

Returning to the Text for Evaluation and Analysis

- Review the partner reading and how they used the strategies to read difficult vocabulary.
- Discuss their likes and dislikes about the recount and why.
- Introduce the sequence words and nouns from Copymaster 5.
- Together, through discussion, sequence the events of the text using the sequence words as the guide. *What happened first? Where did they go? Where does it tell us that? What did they do next?*
- Ensure the group keep referring back to the text for the evidence.

Belfast

Guided Writing

Key Objectives

- Write simple recounts linked to topics of interest/study using the language of texts read as a model for own writing.
- Through reading and writing, reinforce knowledge of the term 'sentence' from previous terms.

Task

Write a sequence of sentences to match the pictures using the structure of the 'Belfast' text.

Each child will need *Our City Holidays* and Copymaster 6.
The teacher will need a whiteboard and marker pen.

Introduction

- Together, reread the 'Belfast' text.
- Tell the children they will need to keep referring to their books for the task.
- Give each child a copy of **Copymaster 6**. Discuss the pictures and ask the group for suitable sentences to match the pictures. Ask questions to remind the group to generate the full sentences. *What always goes at the end of the sentence?*
- Demonstrate the first sentence on the whiteboard, pausing to encourage the children to help with the capital letter, spellings and full stop, e.g. 'I went to _____.' [place of group choice taken from the list generated in the guided reading]. Reread the sentence together.
- Check proper understanding of the task before moving into the writing.

Children Writing Individually

- *Say the sentence quietly to yourself before you start to write.* Remind the children to use their guided reading books to support their writing.
- Tell the children to say each word, separating out the phonemes where appropriate, e.g. 'w-e-n-t'.
- Where it is a high frequency word, children should write the word independently. If there are any difficulties, write the word on your whiteboard and take the child/children through the 'look, say, cover, write, check' process.
- Suggest each child repeats the whole sentence they have written aloud, self-checking for the three elements that make up the sentence structure.

Evaluation

- Each child should read one sentence in sequence to the group.
- Review the use of the sentence structure they have written during the session.
- Reflect on progress made. *Which words can you write now? Which words were difficult?* Volunteers could demonstrate on the whiteboard.

Suggested Independent Activities

- Record on tape your recount of a school visit or holiday.
- With an adult or partner, try to find some more information about Belfast.
- Using the sequence words, write some full sentences about 'a day in my life at school'.

A Visit to Belfast

Belfast
friend
Superbowl
Candy Factory
museum

First
Second
Next
After that
Then

Our City Holidays in ________________

I ____________________ ____________________ We ____________________ ____________________	 cinema
We ____________________ ____________________ We ____________________ ____________________	 clown juggling
We ____________________ ____________________ We ____________________ They ____________________ ____________________	 museum dinosaurs

Liverpool

Guided Reading

Key Objectives

- Read recounts and begin to recognise generic structure, e.g. ordered sequence of events, use of words like 'first', 'next', 'after', 'when'.
- Identify simple questions and use the text to find answers.
- Locate parts of the text that give particular information, including labelled diagrams and charts.

The teacher will need a Beatles song (if possible) and Copymaster 7 cut up and stuck onto separate cards.

Introduction

- Tell the children that they are going to be reading about a visit to Liverpool. Show the children Liverpool on the map in *Our City Holidays*.
- If you happen to have a Beatles' song, play it now as part of the introductory part of the read [especially 'The Magical Mystery Tour'!]
- Support the group in finding page 14. Make sure the children remember that this book is written in the first person. *The child is telling us what they did and who they are with.* Demonstrate by reading the first line of the text: 'I went to Liverpool', 'We went across …'
- Ask the children to work in pairs as they scan the text, paying particular attention to the pictures.
- Go through the text together, using the discussion to draw out the difficult vocabulary.
- **Strategy Check:** Remind the children to use the pictures to help with difficult words. Demonstrate how predicting, leaving a gap and rereading is a useful reading strategy.

Reading and Discussion

- Remind the children of the two strategy prompts before they start to read independently, but one page at a time.
- Support individual readers as necessary.
- After each page, discuss content, words and pictures.
- Continue with the above process for the rest of the text.

Returning to the Text for Evaluation and Analysis

- Discuss what the group can remember about the text.
- Ask each question from Copymaster 7 to check for comprehension. Encourage the group to point to the evidence in the text. *Use the text, pictures and captions.*

Liverpool

Guided Writing

Key Objectives

- Use texts to find answers. Locate parts of text that give particular information.
- Through reading and writing, reinforce knowledge of the term 'sentence' from previous terms.

Task

Locate the answers to the questions. Write the answers in full sentences.

Each child will need *Our City Holidays*, a whiteboard and marker pen, and Copymaster 8.

The teacher will need an enlarged copy of Copymaster 8 and a pen.

Introduction

- Reread the 'Liverpool' text to the group. Point out the pictures and captions.
- Explain the task and give each child a copy of **Copymaster 8**. Talk through what they have to do.
- Use the enlarged copy of **Copymaster 8** and together answer one of the questions. Ask the children to find the evidence in the text. Word the answer in different ways ensuring that each answer is presented as a full sentence.

Children Writing Individually

- When the children are writing the sentences, they should compose each sentence orally and rehearse it with a partner or the teacher before writing.
- Children can use their whiteboards to practise words before writing on their copymasters. Encourage the children to say the words to themselves as they write.
- Tell the children to reread the sentence to make sure it makes sense.

Evaluation

- Allow time for the children to read through their work with the rest of the group. Notice how the same answer can be written in different ways.
- Review the ways the children found the spellings they needed.
- Ask the group to generate some more questions about the 'Liverpool' text. Record them on the enlarged **Copymaster 8**.

Suggested Independent Activities

- Answer the new questions on the enlarged **Copymaster 8**.
- With a partner, find out more information about Liverpool from the Internet or the library.
- Try writing your own set of questions about one of the places you have visited.

Liverpool Questions

Who went to Liverpool?

What did they cross the River Mersey on?

What was the bus tour called?

Where did they find out about the Beatles?

When did they go to the Liverpool Football Club shop?

What I Know About Liverpool

How can you travel across the Mersey?

____

____

What is the bus tour called?

____

____

What is the museum called?

____

____

Where can you go to buy Liverpool Football Club things?

____

____

Edinburgh

Guided Reading

Key Objectives

- Read recounts and begin to recognise generic structure, e.g. ordered sequence of events, use of words like 'first', 'next', 'after', 'when'.
- Locate parts of the text that give particular information, including labelled diagrams and charts.

The teacher will need Copymaster ❾ already cut up and stuck onto separate cards, and a whiteboard and marker pen.

Introduction

- Introduce the book by talking about places the children have visited. Make a list on the whiteboard of names of places that can be used during the guided sessions.
- Look at the front and back covers of the book. Read the title to the group. Establish the content. *This book is about children's visits to lots of different cities in the UK.*
- Show the children the map and find Edinburgh. *This is the city we are reading about today.*
- Give out *Our City Holidays* and ask the children to find page 22. *The title is Edinburgh.* Look through the pictures, captions and text and introduce the unfamiliar vocabulary by showing the cards from **Copymaster ❾** and placing them in the middle of the table.
- *Who is telling the reader about the visit to Edinburgh?* Discuss and clarify with the group.
- **Strategy Check:** Remind the children to use the pictures to help with difficult words. Demonstrate how predicting, leaving a gap and rereading is a useful reading strategy.

Reading and Discussion

- Ask the children to read each page quietly out loud. Refer to the strategy checks.
- Check each child as they read, and prompt and support with strategies as necessary.
- When they have read the text ask children to partner each other – one to be the teacher and the other to read the text. *Help the reader as I have done by reminding them to look at the pictures or predict a word, leave a gap and then reread the sentence.*
- The partners can then take turns to read to each other and play the part of the teacher.

Returning to the Text for Evaluation and Analysis

- Review the partner reading and how they used the strategies to read difficult vocabulary.
- Discuss their likes and dislikes about the recount and why.
- Introduce the sequence questions from **Copymaster ❾**.
- Together, through discussion, sequence the events of the text using sequence words and the nouns on the other cards. *What happened first? Where did they go next? Where does it tell us that? What did they do afterwards?*
- Ensure the group keep referring back to the text for the evidence.

Edinburgh

Guided Writing

Key Objectives

- Use texts to find answers. Locate parts of text that give particular information.
- Through reading and writing, reinforce knowledge of the term 'sentence' from previous terms.

Task

Locate the answers to the questions. Write the answers in full sentences.

Each child will need *Our City Holidays*, a whiteboard and marker pen, and Copymaster 10.
The teacher will need an enlarged copy of Copymaster 10 and a pen.

Introduction

- Together, reread the 'Edinburgh' text.
- Give out **Copymaster 10** and explain the task.
- Use the enlarged copy of **Copymaster 10** and together answer one of the questions. Ask the children to find the evidence in the text. Word the answer in different ways, ensuring that each answer is presented as a full sentence.

Children Writing Individually

- When the children are writing the sentences, they should compose each sentence orally and rehearse it with a partner or the teacher before writing.
- Children can use their whiteboards to practise words before writing on their copymasters. Encourage the children to say the words to themselves as they write.
- Tell the children to reread the sentence to make sure it makes sense.

Evaluation

- Allow time for the children to read through their work with the rest of the group. Notice how the same answer can be written in different ways.
- Review the ways the children found the spellings they needed.
- Ask the group to generate some questions about the 'Edinburgh' text. Record them on the enlarged **Copymaster 10**.

Suggested Independent Activities

- Answer the new questions on the enlarged **Copymaster 10**.
- With a partner, find out more information about Edinburgh from the Internet or the library.
- Try writing your own set of questions about one of the places you have visited.

A Visit to Edinburgh

Edinburgh	Scotland
tower	dungeons
Scott Monument	
Princes Street	
Mons Meg	ramparts
Museum of Childhood	

What happened first?

Where did they go next?

Where did they go shopping?

What did they do afterwards?

What I Know About Edinburgh

What has 287 steps?

____

____

What joins the Old Town to the New Town?

____

____

Where can you have a picnic?

____

____

What is in the Museum of Childhood?

____

____

Birmingham

Guided Reading

Key Objectives

- Read recounts and begin to recognise generic structure, e.g. ordered sequence of events, use of words like 'first', 'next', 'after', 'when'.
- Read simple questions and use the text to find answers.
- Locate parts of the text that give particular information, including labelled diagrams and charts.

Each child will need a copy of Copymaster 11.

The teacher will need an enlarged copy of Copymaster 11.

Introduction

- Tell the children that they will be reading about a visit to Birmingham. Show the children where Birmingham is on the map in the guided reading book and ask them if they can remember where Edinburgh is, from the last reading session.
- Support the group in finding page 26.
- Ask the children to work in pairs as they scan the text, paying particular attention to the pictures.
- Go through the text together, using the discussion to draw out the difficult vocabulary. Ask the children to identify problematic words. Get them to try and work out the words together.
- **Strategy Check:** Remind the children to use the pictures to help with difficult words. Demonstrate how predicting, leaving a gap and rereading is a useful reading strategy.

Reading and Discussion

- Remind the children of the two strategy prompts before they start to read independently, but one page at a time.
- Support individual readers as necessary.
- After each page, discuss content, words and pictures.
- Continue with the above process for the rest of the text.

Returning to the Text for Evaluation and Analysis

- Discuss what the group can remember about the text. Talk about likes and dislikes and compare with things the children might have done.
- Together, ask each question from Copymaster 11 to check for comprehension. Encourage the group to point to the evidence in the text. *Use the text, pictures and captions.* The children should answer orally. The teacher can record them.

Birmingham

Guided Writing

Key Objectives

- Use the language and features of non-fiction texts, e.g. captions for pictures.
- Through reading and writing, reinforce knowledge of the term 'sentence' from previous terms.

Task

Write captions to explain the pictures. The answers should be in full sentences.

Each child will need *Our City Holidays*, a whiteboard and marker pen, and Copymaster 12.
The teacher will need a whiteboard and marker pen.

Introduction

- Reread the 'Birmingham' text to the group. Point out the pictures and captions.
- Give out Copymaster 12 and explain the task. *Write a caption for each of the circus pictures.*
- Use the whiteboard, and together, formulate two or three possible sentences for the first picture. Remind the children of the three elements to check to ensure it is a sentence. [A capital letter, a full stop, and that it makes sense.]

Children Writing Individually

- When the children are writing the sentences, they should compose each sentence orally and rehearse it with a partner or the teacher before writing.
- Children can use their whiteboards to practise words before writing on their copymasters. Encourage the children to say the words to themselves as they write.
- Remind the children to check for mistakes by reading their finished sentence. *Does it make sense? Have you remembered the capital letter and the full stop?*

Evaluation

- Allow time for the children to read through their work with the rest of the group. Notice how the same explanations can be written in different ways.
- Review the ways the children found the spellings they needed.
- Ask the children to share one of their captions with the rest of the group.

Suggested Independent Activities

- Write a mini book of a visit you have made. Use sentences, pictures and captions.
- With a partner, find out more information about Birmingham from the Internet or the library.
- With a partner, read about some of the other visits in *Our City Holidays*.

Birmingham Questions

What is made at the factory?

How many films were showing at Star City?

What did they see at the Sea Life Centre?

Where did they go for a ride on a boat?

What two things did they see at the science museum?